max science primary

Workook 2

DISCOVERING THROUGH ENQUIRY

PAT DOWER

SERIES EDITOR: BOB KIBBLE

macmillan education

INTERNATIONAL CURRICULUM

Macmillan Education
4 Crinan Street
London N1 9XW
A division of Springer Nature Limited

Companies and representatives throughout the world

Workbook ISBN 978-1-380-02156-4

First published 2019

Original design by EMC Design Ltd and Macmillan Education
Page make-up by Ink Design
Illustrated by Magriet Brink pp 4, 5; Lynda Ward pp 2, 12, 27, 56, 57, 58, 60, 65; Sean Strydom pp 13, 17, 23, 33, 34; Tamsin Hinrichsen pp 7, 19, 62
Cover design by Sparks Publishing Services Ltd and Macmillan Education
Cover illustration by Star Publishing Pte Ltd and Jorge Santillan c/o Beehive Illustration Agency
Picture research by Susannah Jayes

The author and publishers would like to thank the following for permission to reproduce their photographs:
Getty Images/Westend61 p3.

Printed and bound in Brazil
2024
22

Contents

Introducing the *Max Science primary* Workbook

The *Max Science primary* Workbooks accompany the Student Book for class and home use. All the numbered activities and extension activities found in the Student Book are expanded with clear answer spaces and support. Instructions carefully show if activities are to be done independently, in pairs or in groups.

Practising my science language

Supported activities focus on improving scientific literacy to make the learning of science through the medium of English more accessible.

Extending understanding

Extension questions encourage learners to go a bit further to improve the depth of understanding.

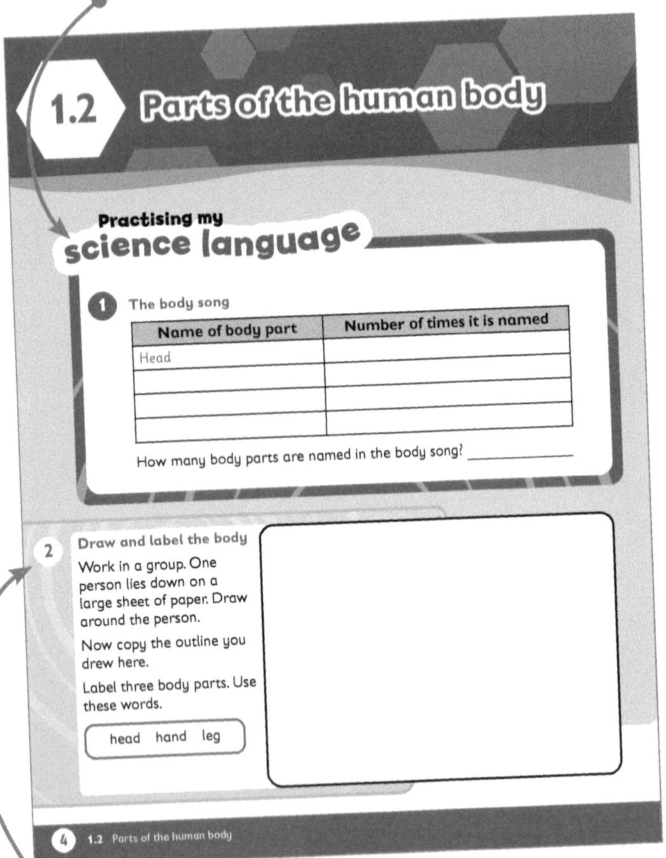

1.2 Parts of the human body

Practising my science language

1 The body song

Name of body part	Number of times it is named
Head	

How many body parts are named in the body song? ____________

2 Draw and label the body

Work in a group. One person lies down on a large sheet of paper. Draw around the person.

Now copy the outline you drew here.

Label three body parts. Use these words.

head hand leg

4 1.2 Parts of the human body

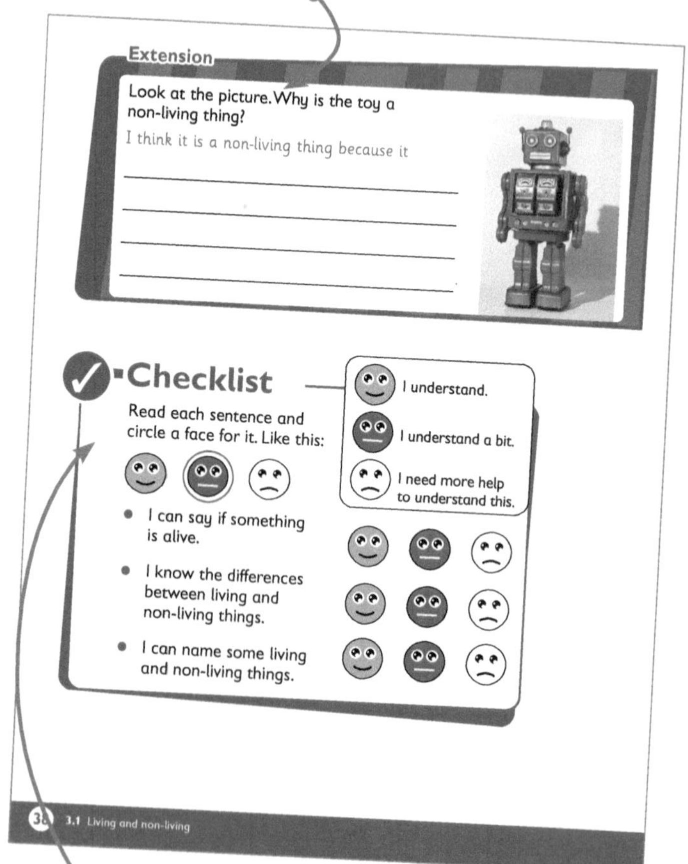

Extension

Look at the picture. Why is the toy a non-living thing?

I think it is a non-living thing because it

Checklist

Read each sentence and circle a face for it. Like this:

I understand.

I understand a bit.

I need more help to understand this.

- I can say if something is alive.
- I know the differences between living and non-living things.
- I can name some living and non-living things.

38 3.1 Living and non-living

Exploring science further

Numbered activities from the Student Book are expanded with example answers for guidance. Learners can record their scientific progress, insights and results.

Assessing progress

End of topic checklists provide opportunities for recording what learners have learnt so far.

1.1 Where does light come from?

1 Exploring where light comes from

Look at the objects that your teacher has put around the room.

Draw a tick next to the objects that give off light.

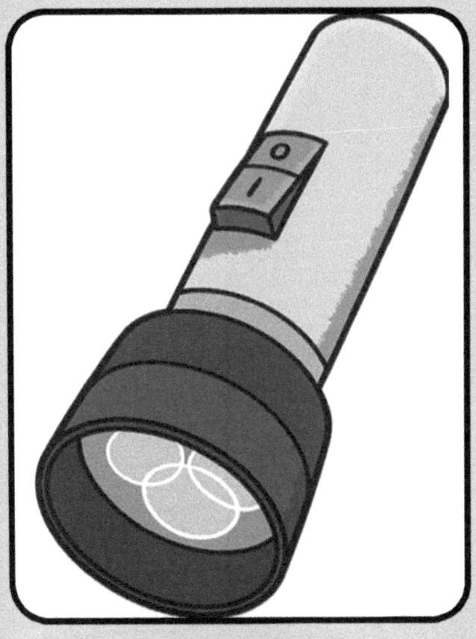

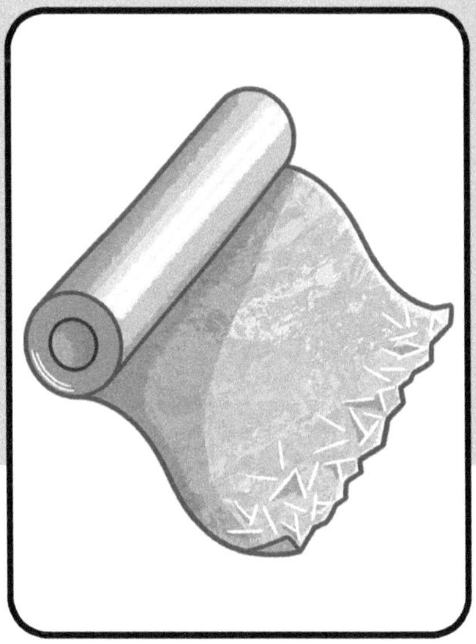

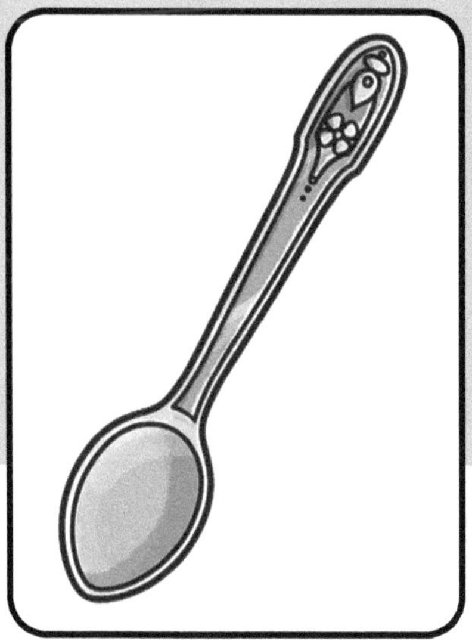

2 Investigating further

Take the objects from Activity 1 into a dark place.

Which objects give off their own light?

Which objects do not give off their own light?

Complete the table. One has been done for you.

Objects that give off their own light	Objects that do not give off their own light
torch	

Look again at your answers in Activity 1.

Did you change your mind for any of the objects?

If so, why?

I changed my mind because ______________________________

____

____

____.

3 **Looking at flames**

Look at a burning candle.

What colours can you see? What movement can you see?

Draw the candle's flame below. Colour it in.

Label the brighter and dimmer parts of the flame.

Look at your Student Book and listen to your teacher who will give you ideas. Write some words to describe the candle flame.

____

____

Extension

Look at the teaspoons in the picture.

Why do you think one teaspoon looks brighter than the other?

One teaspoon is brighter because ______________

____

____.

1.2 Light and dark

1 **Looking for complete darkness**

Look at the picture in the Student Book on page 8. There is light coming from the head torch.

What happens if the head torch is switched off?

2 **The dark box**

Will you be able to see these objects in a dark place? Circle your guesses.

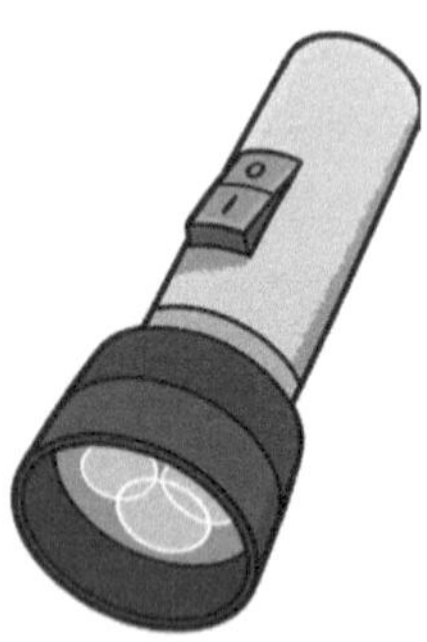

Yes No

Yes No

Yes No

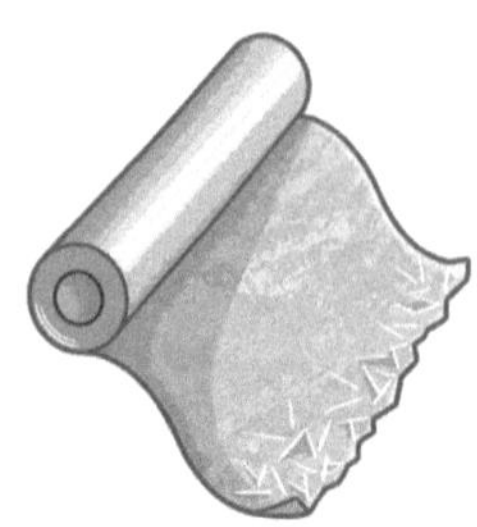

Yes No

Now put the different objects in the dark box. Which objects can you see? Which guesses were right? Tell your partner.

Extension

Martha uses a candle to help her to read in the dark.

Martha has a mirror.

She can see the real candle and the candle in the mirror.

This means that Martha can see two candles.

Does this make the room brighter than with only the real candle?

Circle your answer: **Yes** **No**

3 **Can you see a white rabbit in a very dark room?**

Snowy is a white rabbit.

Trace Snowy's shape onto white paper. Cut it out.

Turn on a light in a small room or cupboard.

Fix the paper rabbit to the wall.

If you turn the light off, it will be very, very dark.

Can you see Snowy? **Yes** **No**

Can you see anything? **Yes** **No**

Why? Complete this sentence:

I ______________ see Snowy when ______________________________.

Checklist

I understand.

I understand a bit.

I need more help to understand this.

Read each sentence and circle a face for it. Like this:

- I can name things that give off their own light.
- I know some objects only pass on light from elsewhere.
- I can describe what "dark" means.
- I can describe the difference between bright light, dim light and darkness.

1.3 Shadows

1 **Amar's shadow**

Amar has lost his shadow. Draw Amar's shadow for him.

2 **Looking at my shadow**

Go outside on a sunny day and look at your shadow.

Is your shadow completely dark? **Yes** **No**

Can you see your face in your shadow? **Yes** **No**

Now look back at your drawing of Amar's shadow in Activity 1. Draw your own shadow. Have you drawn it in a different way to Amar's shadow?

Extension

Go outside on a cloudy day. Look for your shadow. Write what you see here:

____

____

3 **What makes a shadow?**

In the space, draw the shadow that you made.

Practising my science language

4 **Helping Eva to understand shadows**

Talk about these sentences in a group.

Make a tick for a sentence that is correct.

Make a cross to show that a sentence is incorrect.

- My shadow is black. ☐
- I have a shadow when it is completely dark. ☐
- I have a shadow when light is shining. ☐
- I can make a shadow by putting something in the way of a shining light. ☐
- All objects have the same shadow. ☐

Rewrite the incorrect sentences so that they are correct:

____

____

____

Checklist

Read each sentence and circle a face for it. Like this:

I understand.

I understand a bit.

I need more help to understand this.

- I know what a shadow is.
- I can draw shadows correctly.
- I can say what makes shadows.

Glossary

Fill in the meaning of these words in your own language.

dark

shadow

light

Sun

shade

torch

2.1 What does a battery do?

1 Which objects need a battery?

Tick the objects that need batteries to make them work. One has been done for you.

 ☐

 ☐

 ☐

 ☐

 ☐

 ☑

Choose one object that does not need a battery to work.

I chose the ______________________________.

How does it work?

____

____

2 Looking at batteries

Look at the batteries your teacher shows you.

Circle "Yes" or "No" at each question to say what detail you see:

- Can you see a + and a — on every battery? **Yes** **No**
- Are the numbers or letters the same on each battery? **Yes** **No**
- Do all batteries have metal ends? **Yes** **No**

Now colour in the pictures so that they look like the batteries you looked at.

Draw some of the detail you saw on each of these batteries.

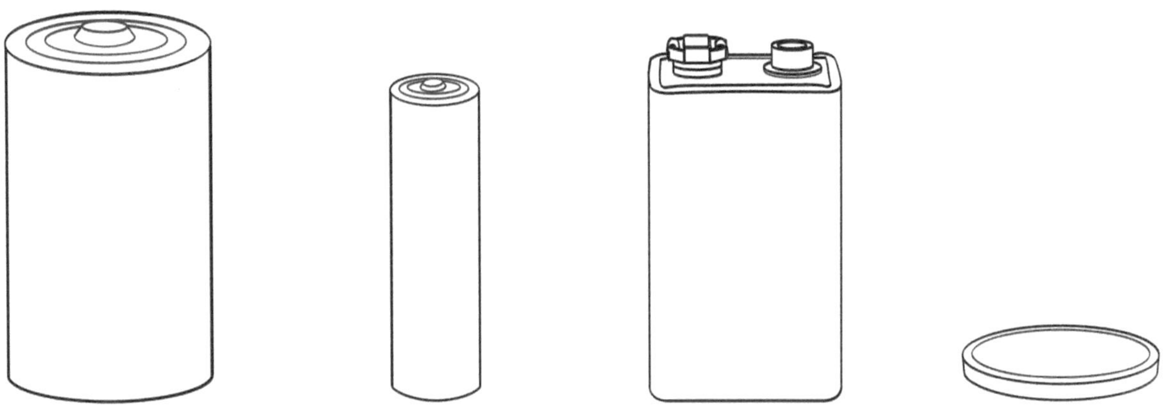

Compare two of these batteries.

- Write one thing that is the same.

The batteries look the same because they ______________________________

____.

- Write one thing that is different.

The batteries look different because ______________________________

____.

3 Looking at light bulbs and bulb holders

Look carefully at the light bulb and bulb holder. Draw the light bulb.

What can you see inside the light bulb?

I can see ____________________________________.

What is the job of the bulb holder?

The bulb holder ____________________________________.

Extension

Why do you think the filament in a bulb can break?

____

Practising my
science language

4 Completing a circuit

Draw a picture to show your completed circuit.

Use words from the box to label the parts of the circuit.

wire	battery	bulb

Complete these sentences to describe your circuit.

Use words from the box.

bulb	complete	wires	light
circuit	electricity	battery	connect

The wires are used to _ _ _ _ _ _ _ the bulb to the battery.

The battery gives _ _ _ _ _ _ _ _ _ _ _ to the bulb.

The electricity flows through the _ _ _ _ _, the bulb and then back to the battery.

This path is called a _ _ _ _ _ _ _.

To make the bulb light up the circuit must be

_ _ _ _ _ _ _ _.

Checklist

Read each sentence and circle a face for it. Like this:

I understand.

I understand a bit.

I need more help to understand this.

- I can name some things that need electricity to work.
- I can say what a battery does.
- I know the parts of a circuit.
- I can build a circuit.
- I can say why a circuit must be complete for a bulb to light up.

2.2 Exploring circuits

1 **Which circuit will work?**

Only one of the circuits below will work. Predict which circuit will light up the bulb. Colour in the bulb in this circuit.

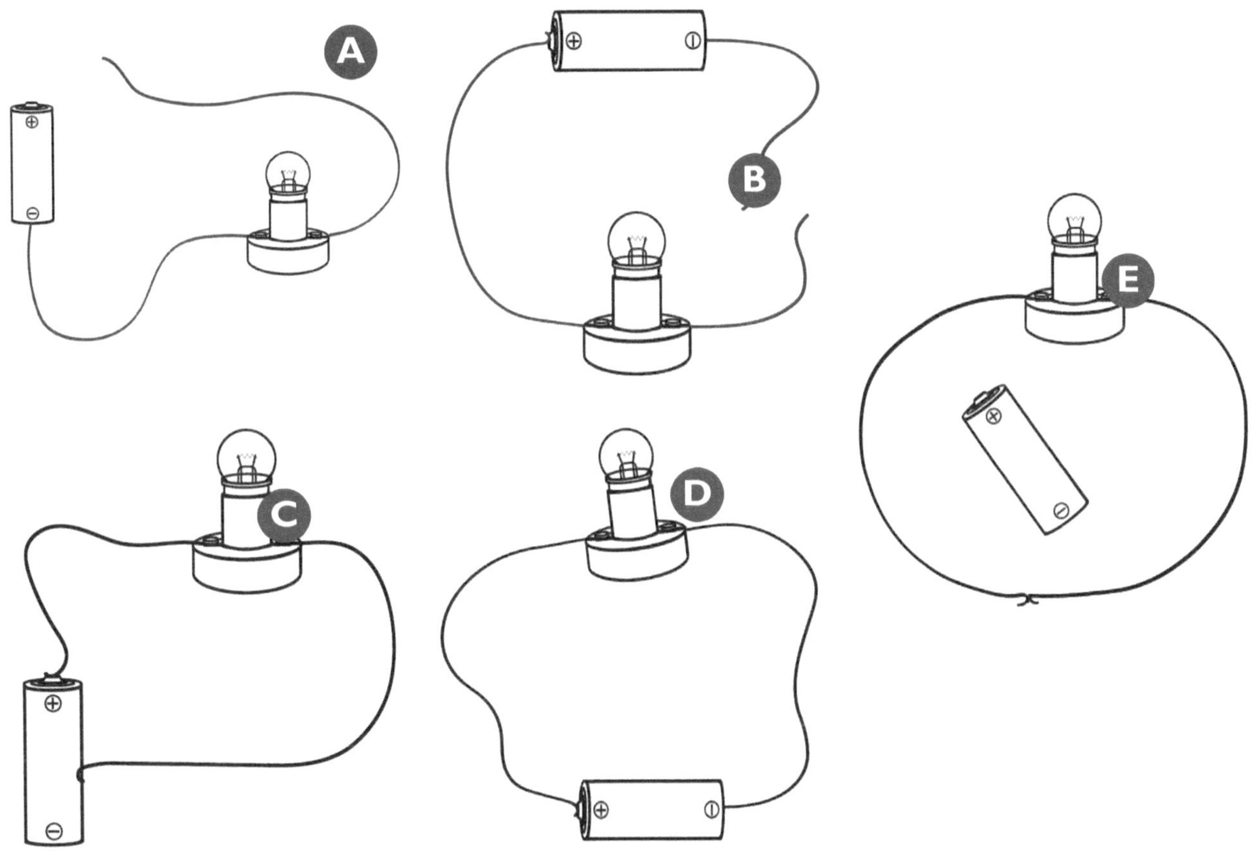

Test your prediction by using a battery, a bulb and wires to build the circuits.

Do you have different ideas now? Write your new ideas here.

____

____

____

Extension

Use wires of different colours to make a circuit.

Does the colour of the wires make any difference to how the circuit works? **Yes** **No**

What material is inside each wire?

____

2 **Testing Toby's idea**

Toby has a bulb, wires and a battery, but he does not have a bulb holder.

Toby thinks he can still make the bulb light up.

Do you agree with Toby? **Yes** **No**

Explain why you say so. ______________________________

____

Test your idea. Were you right? **Yes** **No**

Practising my science language

3 **Making a cosmic energy ball light up**

Read the sentences below to say how to make the cosmic energy ball work. In each sentence, circle the correct word in **bold**.

- There is a **bell** / **bulb** inside the ball.
- The ball works with **movement** / **electricity**.
- When everyone holds hands, we make a **circuit** / **circle**.
- If we do not hold hands, the **wires** / **electricity** cannot flow around the **circuit** / **ball**.

4 **Playing circuits**

Let one learner wear the battery hat. Let another learner wear the light bulb hat.

Stand in a circle to play the circuit game. Your teacher will explain how the game works.

Circuit 1

Circuit 2

- In Circuit 1 you should all hold hands.
- In Circuit 2 you should all hold the rope.

What happens when two people are not holding hands in Circuit 1?

____

____

____

What happens if one person is not touching the rope in Circuit 2?

____

____

____

Extension

Try to draw a circuit that will make two bulbs light up at the same time.

Checklist

I understand.

I understand a bit.

I need more help to understand this.

Read each sentence and circle a face for it. Like this:

- I can connect a battery and bulb to make the bulb light up.
- I can predict when a circuit will make a bulb light up.
- I can test my predictions.
- I know that electricity flows in a complete circuit.

2.3 Switches and staying safe

1 **A switch in a circuit**

Draw a circuit with a bulb and a switch.

How can you use the switch to turn the bulb on or off?

____

____

Draw a circuit with a buzzer and a switch.

How can you use the switch to turn the buzzer on or off?

____

____

2 **How does a switch work?**

How does a switch start or stop the flow of electricity? Circle the right word in each sentence:

- When I **open** / **close** the switch, electricity flows around the circuit. The bulb lights up.
- When I **open** / **close** the switch, electricity does not flow around the circuit. The bulb does not light up.

3

Looking for switches and sockets

Remember, electricity can be **dangerous**. Do not touch the switches or sockets unless your teacher says it is safe.

List three things that the switches do.

___

___

___

What are the sockets used for?

___

___

4

Making an alarm

Draw a picture to show how you think Tya's alarm should work.

Complete these sentences by choosing the best ending for each one from the word box.

the box is opened   make a noise
the alarm to sound   tell me that the box has been opened
electricity to flow through the buzzer   the circuit is complete

The alarm has a buzzer to ______________________________

____.

The buzzer sounds when ______________________________

____.

A complete circuit is needed for ______________________________

____.

Extension

Tick the circuits below that will make the buzzer sound when the switch is closed.

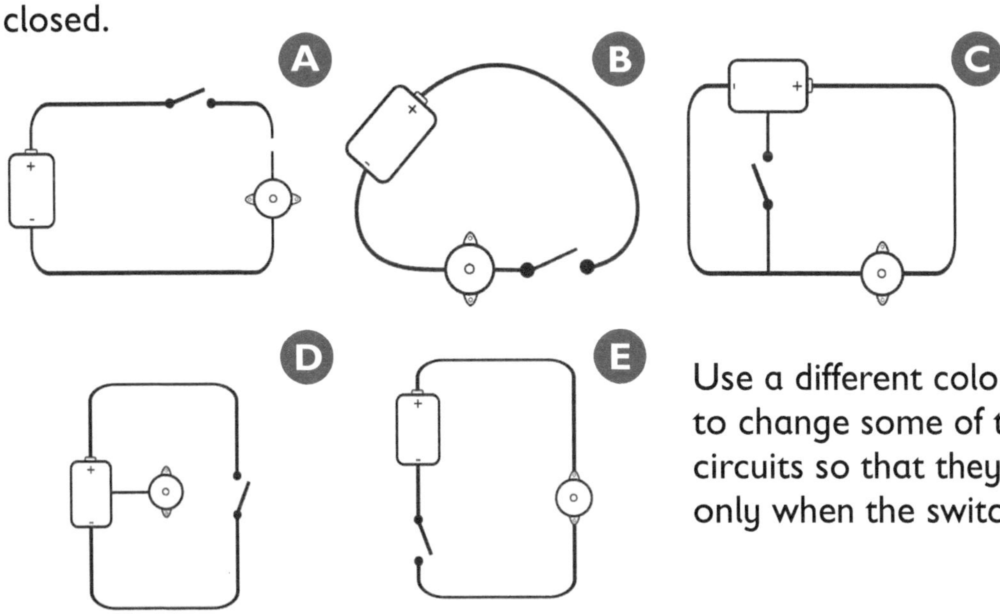

Use a different coloured pencil to change some of the other circuits so that they will work only when the switch is closed.

Practising my science language

5 A safety slogan

Draw a poster to warn people that electricity is dangerous.

Write your own slogan for the poster. You can use the words in the word box to help you.

Be careful ...	Do not ...	Remember ...
Take care ...	Keep away from ...	

Checklist

I understand.

I understand a bit.

I need more help to understand this.

Read each sentence and circle a face for it. Like this:

- I can find different kinds of switches.
- I can make a circuit with a switch.
- I know how a switch turns something on or off.
- I know that electricity can be dangerous.
- I know some ways to stay safe when using electricity.

Glossary

Fill in the meaning of these words in your own language.

battery

battery holder

bulb

buzzer

cell

circuit

connect

connector

dangerous

electricity

filament

flow

lamp

socket

switch

wire

3.1 Changing shape

1 Changing the shape of modelling clay

Make four balls of modelling clay.

Draw the shape of one of the balls.

Change the shape of each ball of modelling clay by:

- squashing it
- twisting it
- stretching it
- bending it.

Draw the new shape of each ball of modelling clay. Write down what action you used to make each one. An example has been done for you.

Action: Squashing 	**Action:** ______________
Action: ______________	**Action:** ______________

Extension

Make a model of your favourite animal with the modelling clay.

Draw the animal you made. Write the name of the animal on your drawing.

What actions did you use to change the shape of the clay? Choose some words from the box.

squashing	bending	pushing	pulling
twisting	turning	stretching	

I changed the shape of the clay by ______________________________

____.

2 Do all materials change shape?

Work in a pair.

Look at the pictures on page 32 of the Student Book.

- What material is each object made from?
- Predict which materials will change shape.
- Then test your predictions. Were your predictions correct?

Show your answers in the table. Make a cross for "No". Make a tick for "Yes".

One example has been done for you.

Object	Material	Will it change shape? (✓ or ✗)	Did it change shape? (✓ or ✗)	Was your prediction correct? (✓ or ✗)
Table	Wood	✗	✗	✓

Extension

In a group, talk about the picture in the Student Book on page 33. Write some of your ideas here.

- What shape do you think the track used to have?

___

___

- What do you think caused the shape to change?

___

___

Checklist

🙂	I understand.
😐	I understand a bit.
🙁	I need more help to understand this.

Read each sentence and circle a face for it. Like this:

- I can say how a material's shape can change.
- I can predict whether a material's shape will change.
- I can test my predictions.

3.2 Can heating or cooling change materials?

1 Cooling materials

Work in a group.

Your teacher will give you some materials.

Choose one of these words to describe what each material is like. Fill in the table together.

hard soft runny

Material	What is it like at the start?	What is it like when it is cool?	What is it like when it is very cold?
Sand			
Water			
Modelling clay			
Cooking oil			
Dry biscuit			

Look at your answers in the table.

Have the materials changed? Circle the correct words in the sentences below.

One has been done for you.

Sand **changes** / **does not change** when it is very cold.

Describe any changes you can see or feel:

____

____

Water **changes** / **does not change** when it is very cold.

Describe any changes you can see or feel:

____

____

Modelling clay **changes** / **does not change** when it is very cold.

Describe any changes you can see or feel:

____

____

Cooking oil **changes** / **does not change** when it is very cold.

Describe any changes you can see or feel:

____

____

A dry biscuit **changes** / **does not change** when it is very cold.

Describe any changes you can see or feel:

____

____

Do all the materials change in the same way when they are cold?

Yes **No**

2 Predicting changes in materials

Think about what the materials in Activity 1 were like when they were very cold.

Predict what will happen when the materials warm up again. Write your answers below.

- When **sand** is warmed again, I think it will ____.
- When **water** is warmed again, I think it will ____.
- When **modelling clay** is warmed again, I think it will ____.
- When **cooking oil** is warmed again, I think it will ____.
- When a **dry biscuit** is warmed again, I think it will ____.

Practising my science language

3 What happens when you heat water?

Your teacher will show you a container of cold water.

Look at the water level marked on the container.

Your teacher will then start to heat the water.

continued on following page ...

... continued from previous page

What can you see in the air above the water?

I can see ______________________________

______________________________.

Has the water level changed? **Yes** **No**

What do you think happened to the water? Write one sentence.

____

Share your sentence with your partner.

4 Collecting tiny water droplets from the air

Think back to what happens when water is heated.

Do you think we can collect the tiny water droplets from the air? **Yes** **No**

What happens when a cold tile is held over the water?

Draw what you can see on the tile.

Tell your partner why you think this happens.

5 Investigating melting

Look at the ideas given below. Circle what you think about each idea.

"Perhaps we can wrap it in paper."

Does not make a difference. / Makes the soup melt fast. / Makes the soup melt slowly.

"We could put a hat over it."

Does not make a difference. / Makes the soup melt fast. / Makes the soup melt slowly.

"We could put it on something hot."

Does not make a difference. / Makes the soup melt fast. / Makes the soup melt slowly.

What else can Kate do to make the frozen soup melt?

____

____

Extension

How can Tom get his soup to cool down? Think of two ideas.

- Tom can ____________________________________
  ____.
- Tom can ____________________________________
  ____.

6 **How do materials change when they are baked?**

Look at some modelling clay and dough before they are baked in an oven.

Can you change the shape of the materials?

Break off a piece of modelling clay and a piece of dough. What is each material like inside?

Your teacher will now bake the clay and dough.

Fill in the table below to describe what you found out:

- Make a tick if the description is true.
- Make a cross if the description is not true.

One has been done for you.

	Unbaked clay	Baked clay	Unbaked dough	Baked dough
I can change its shape.	✓			
It is soft.				
It is hard.				
It is solid inside.				
It is fluffy inside.				

Extension

Try mixing the baked modelling clay and the baked dough with some water.

Can baked modelling clay change back into soft clay? **Yes** **No**

What happened when you added water?

____

Can baked dough change back into unbaked dough? **Yes** **No**

What happened when you added water?

____

Checklist

Read each sentence and circle a face for it. Like this:

I understand.

I understand a bit.

I need more help to understand this.

- I know that heating or cooling a material can make it change.
- I can say how water changes when it is heated or cooled.
- I know that some solid materials can melt when they get hot.
- I can investigate how to make a material melt fast or slowly.
- I can record and compare my observations.

3.3 Dissolving

1 **Sugar and water**

Place one spoonful of sugar into a glass of water. Do not stir.

Draw what you can see.

Before stirring:

Now stir the sugar and water.

Draw what you can see.

After stirring:

What has happened to the sugar after stirring?

____

Is the sugar still there? **Yes** **No**

Predict what you think the water will taste like.

The water will taste _______________________________.

Hint:

Never taste anything in Science class unless your teacher says it is safe.

2 Which materials dissolve?

Work in a group.

Mix each material into water.

You will need a fresh glass of water for each one.

Tick the materials that dissolve:

Baking powder	☐	Pebbles	☐
Chalk	☐	Powder paint	☐
Flour	☐	Salt	☐
Glass beads	☐	Sand	☐
Instant coffee	☐	Sawdust	☐

Practising my science language

3 Results table

Record your results from Activity 2 in the table below. One has been done for you.

Materials that dissolve	Materials that do not dissolve
	chalk

Think about what you have learnt about dissolving. Try to write two sentences using the words listed below. You can use the words more than once.

dissolve water stir salt sand

continued on following page …

… continued from previous page

Write your sentences here:

1 ______________________________

____

2 ______________________________

____

4 **Does a sugar lump dissolve as easily as sugar granules?**

Place a sugar cube in a glass of water. Stir the water gently for five counts.

Place a spoonful of sugar granules in another glass of water. Stir the water gently for five counts.

How well did each type of sugar dissolve? Make a tick mark in the right box in the table.

	It dissolved a lot	It dissolved a little bit	It did not dissolve at all
Sugar cube			
Sugar granules			

Extension

Work with your partner.

Get a glass of cold water. Also get a glass of warm water.

The glasses should be the same size. They should be filled to the same level.

continued on following page …

Extension continued

Your teacher will give you two identical tablets.

- Drop one tablet into the cold water. Count out loud to measure how long it takes to dissolve. ______________
- Now drop the other tablet into the warm water. How many counts does it take to dissolve? ______________

In which glass does the tablet dissolve faster?

Warm water **Cold water**

Is this a fair test? **Yes** **No**

Why do you say so?

____

____

Checklist

I understand.

I understand a bit.

I need more help to understand this.

Read each sentence and circle a face for it. Like this:

- I can say what happens when a material dissolves.
- I can investigate whether a material dissolves or not.
- I can record my results in a table.
- I can name some materials that dissolve.

3.4 Natural and man-made materials

1 **Where do these materials come from?**

Look at the natural materials your teacher gives you. Where do they come from?

Work with your partner to fill in the table. An example has been done for you.

From a plant	From an animal	From the ground
	leather	

Practising my science language

2 **Uses of some man-made materials**

Look at the pictures of man-made materials on page 43 of your Student Book. Complete the sentences about the following materials.

An example has been done for you.

- Crude oil is used to make fuel for cars.
- Steel is used to make ____________________.
- Plastic is used to make ____________________.
- Glass is used to make ____________________.

3 **Natural and man-made materials**

Work in a group.

Draw an outline map of your school. Label the places.

Where did you find **natural materials**? Make a green "N" at these places.

Where did you find **man-made materials**? Make a black "M" at these places.

4 **Natural and man-made materials on display**

Name one natural material on the poster: ____________________

____

Name one man-made material on the poster: ____________________

____

Extension

Name two objects that are made from natural materials.

Object 1: __________ Object 2: __________

Material: __________ Material: __________

What has been done to each material to make the objects?

Object 1: ____

____

Object 2: ____

____

Checklist

Read each sentence and circle a face for it. Like this:

- I understand.
- I understand a bit.
- I need more help to understand this.

- I can name some natural materials.
- I can say what "man-made" means.
- I can name some man-made materials.

Glossary

In your own language, write down what these words mean:

bend

change

cool

dissolve

heat

irreversible

man-made

material

melt

natural

results table

reversible

rigid

shape

solid

squash

Glossary

stretch

____

____

twist

____

____

water droplets

____

____

4.1 Different types of rock

1 **Hunting for rocks**

How many different types of rock did you find?

I found ____________________ different types of rock.

2 **Looking at and describing rocks**

Listen to your partner describe a rock. They must not show you the rock.

Draw a picture of what they describe.

Now look at the rock. Tick one phrase below that best describes your drawing.

It looks nearly the same as the rock. ☐

It looks quite similar to the rock. ☐

It does not look much like the rock. ☐

3 Sorting rocks

Look at the rocks you found.

What features can you see? Circle your answers below.

Rough or **smooth** **Shiny** or **dull** **Hard** or **soft**

Describe one other feature that you can see in your rocks.

____

Choose two features to sort your rocks into groups. How many rocks are in each group?

Group 1: __________ Group 2: __________

Practising my science language

4 Comparing pebbles, sand and soil

Write words to describe the pebbles, sand and soil in the table below. Some of the words in the word box will help you.

dull	sandy	hard	rough	soft	round	moist
small	smooth	shiny	light	large	dry	dark

Pebbles	Sand	Soil

5 Testing the hardness of rocks

Draw the two rocks your teacher gives you.

Rock 1:

Rock 2:

What do the surfaces feel like?

Rock 1: ______________________________

Rock 2: ______________________________

What happens when you rub the two rocks together?

____

Write "**harder**" or "**softer**" under the correct drawings.

Extension

Test the hardness of each rock by scratching it with a piece of metal.

List the rocks from softest to hardest.

Softest **Hardest**

____

Were any of the rocks the same hardness? **Yes** **No**

Practising my science language

6 **Volcanoes**

Circle the words below that describe the rock when it flows from a volcano.

solid   runny   soft   cold   hard   hot

What is the rock like when it has cooled down?

When the rock has cooled down, it is ______________________

____.

Checklist

Read each sentence and circle a face for it. Like this:

- I understand.
- I understand a bit.
- I need more help to understand this.

- I can compare different types of rock.
- I can compare pebbles, sand and soil.
- I can test how hard a rock is.
- I know of one way that new rocks can form.

4.2 Natural and man-made building materials

1 **Building a pebble wall**

Draw a picture of the dry-stone wall you built.

- Measure how high your wall is.

My wall is ______________ cm high.

Circle your answers.

- How strong is your wall? **Very strong** **Not very strong**
- Can you blow your wall over? **Yes** **No**
- Will it stand up to a strong wind? **Yes** **No**
- What happens when you lean something against the wall?

____

- How can you make your wall stronger?

I can make my wall stronger by ______________________

____.

2 **Building a stone wall with bonding material**

Draw pictures to show the different stages of building your wall.

Colour in the bonding material.

Stage 1	**Stage 2**
Stage 3	**Finished wall**

Compare this wall with the pebble one you built with no bonding material. Circle your answer.

Which wall is higher?	**Wall 1**	**Wall 2**
Which wall is stronger?	**Wall 1**	**Wall 2**

Why does it help to use a bonding material when you build a wall?

____

Practising my science language

3 Making bricks

dry	hard	wet	cold	soft	strong

What is the clay like before it is baked?

Write one sentence. Use some of the words in the word box.

____

What do you think the bricks will be like once the clay is baked?

The bricks will be _______________________________

____.

4 Building a wall with bricks

Draw a picture of the strongest wall.

What helped to make this wall stronger than the other one?

____

Extension

Complete each sentence using the correct ending listed below.

Sometimes people use natural building materials because

____.

Sometimes people use man-made building materials because

____.

...the materials cost a lot of money.

...the materials are easy to build with.

...they can find the materials near where they live.

Checklist

Read each sentence and circle a face for it. Like this:

I understand.

I understand a bit.

I need more help to understand this.

- I can say how to build a strong wall.
- I can name some natural and some man-made building materials.
- I can compare natural and man-made building materials.

Glossary

In your own language, write down what these words mean:

bonding material

building material

group

liquid

man-made

natural

rock

sample

sand

sandy

soil

stone

5.1 Looking for shadows

1 **Where is the Sun?**

Look at the girl and her shadow in the picture.

Tick one of the boxes to show where you think the Sun is.

2 Measuring my shadow

Work with a partner. Make a body shadow at three different times of the day:

- once in the morning
- once in the middle of the day
- once in the afternoon.

Stand still to make a shadow.

Ask your partner to measure your shadow.

Write the time of day and the length of your shadow in the table below.

Remember to also write the units of your measurement.

Time of day			
Length of shadow			

Will it be a fair test if you measure a different person's shadow each time? **Yes** **No**

Write why you think so here: ____

____

Extension

Circle the correct unit to measure:

- how long it takes a runner to finish a race

Litres **Minutes** **Kilograms**

- how much you weigh

Litres **Minutes** **Kilograms**

- how much milk is in a container.

Litres **Minutes** **Kilograms**

Practising my science language

3 A shadow experiment

Go to the playground with a friend.
Take a piece of chalk with you.

Ask your friend to stand still in a sunny place.

Use the chalk to draw around your friend's feet and their shadow.

Write the time on the ground.

Go outside again an hour later.
Ask your friend to stand in the same place.
Draw around their new shadow.

Write the new time.

What has happened to your friend's shadow? Circle your answer.

After 1 hour the shadow got **shorter/longer** and **moved/ did not move**.

Repeat this shadow task three more times throughout the day.

Choose the correct word from the list below to complete these sentences.

objects	longer	measured	moves

- My friend's shadow ___________ during the day even if they stand still.
- Shadows get ___________ in the afternoon.
- We ___________ how long our shadows were.
- Big ___________ have big shadows.

Practise saying the sentences to your partner.

Listen to your partner say the sentences.

5.2 Sundials for telling the time

Practising my science language

1 **Making a sundial**

What time does your sundial show when you first set it up?

____

What time does your sundial show when you look at it again later?

____

Write two sentences about your sundial. Try to use the words in the word box.

shadow	Sun	move

____

____

____

Extension

Find some pictures of different sundials. Copy or stick them in the space.

2 The shadow song

Look at the boy in the picture below.
Draw where you think his shadow should be.

Checklist

Read each sentence and circle a face for it. Like this:

- I understand.
- I understand a bit.
- I need more help to understand this.

- I can say how the position and size of a shadow change during the day.
- I understand how the Sun's position causes shadows to change during the day.
- I know how a sundial works.
- I can make my own sundial.

5.3 Spinning Earth

1 **Making a model**

Label the picture using the words in the box.

Sun	Earth	night-time	daytime

Practising my science language

2 **A model for night and day**

Look at the model for night and day. Then complete these sentences.

Light from the Sun shines onto ______________________________

______________________________.

The light only reaches the side of the Earth that is ______________

______________________________.

The side of the Earth facing away from the Sun ______________

______________________________.

When the Earth turns ______________________________

______________________________.

Now swap your book with your partner. Do you have the same answers?

Extension

What do you think will happen if the Earth stops spinning?

Tick the statements you think are true.

- All parts of the Earth will have only day. ☐
- All parts of the Earth will have only night. ☐
- One half of the Earth will always have day. ☐
- One half of the Earth will always have night. ☐
- Night and day will be just like it is now. ☐

3 **Who is right?**

Read the children's ideas and the clues in the Student Book on pages 67 and 68.

Do you think Mira is correct?		**Yes**		**No**	
Circle which clue helped you decide.	**1**		**2**		**3**
Do you think Ruth is correct?		**Yes**		**No**	
Circle which clue helped you decide.	**1**		**2**		**3**
Do you think Natalie is correct?		**Yes**		**No**	
Circle which clue helped you decide.	**1**		**2**		**3**

Can you now explain the reason for day and night? Write two sentences.

____

____

____

Checklist

I understand.

I understand a bit.

I need more help to understand this.

Read each sentence and circle a face for it. Like this:

- I can say how the Earth moves so that we have day and night.
- I can use clues to help me work out why we have day and night.
- I can use a model to show why we have day and night.

5.4 The Moon

1 **Looking at the Moon**

Write who in your class plays the part of the Earth, the Moon and the Sun.

- ________________ plays the part of the Earth.
- ________________ plays the part of the Moon.
- ________________ plays the part of the Sun.

Look at the picture. What will Layla see when the Moon is in the different positions?

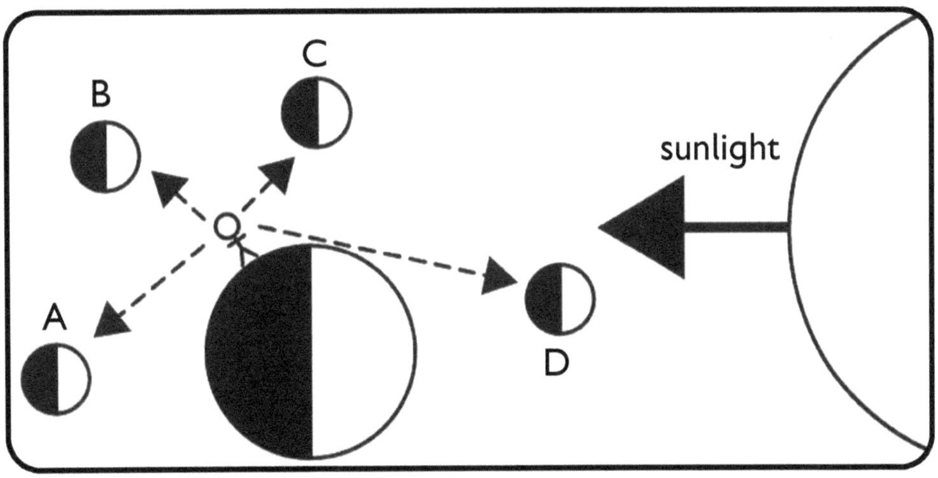

Complete the table below using these symbols:

◇ if she can see a part of the Moon's face

✓ if she can see the whole face of the Moon

✗ if she cannot see the Moon's face at all.

One has been done for you.

Moon in position A	Moon in position B	Moon in position C	Moon in position D
		◇	

Practising my science language

2 **A bigger model for the Moon, Earth and Sun**

Find an open space in the school hall or in the playground.

Use a large, round object to be the Sun.

Use smaller balls for the Earth and Moon.

Make your moving model.

Tick the sentences that describe the movement of the Moon and the Earth correctly. One has been done for you.

- The Moon goes around the Earth. ☐
- The Earth goes around the Moon. ☐
- The Earth goes around the Sun. ☐
- The Earth spins. ☑
- The Earth stays still. ☐
- The Sun goes around the Earth. ☐

Extension

You can see the Sun and the Moon in the sky. The Sun is a star.

Is the Moon also a star?

Talk to your partner. Write your ideas here.

Checklist

Read each sentence and circle a face for it. Like this:

- I understand.
- I understand a bit.
- I need more help to understand this.

- I know that the Moon does not always look the same.
- I understand why the Moon does not always look the same.
- I can describe how the Moon moves.

Glossary

In your own language, write down what these words mean:

axis

dark

day

Earth

equator

globe

light

model

Moon

night

position

shadow

spin

Sun

Glossary

sundial

____

____

torch

____

____

time

____

____

unit

____

____

6.1 Habitats

Practising my science language

1 **Looking for different habitats**

For this activity, you will be learning outside. Take the right clothing: it might be wet, cold or very sunny.

Write about the two habitats. You can write in English or in your own language.

- Name the habitats you explored.
- What animals and plants did you find?

	Name of habitat 1: ____________	Name of habitat 2: ____________
Animals found		
Plants found		

Practising my

science language

2 **What is it like in different habitats?**

Describe the two habitats that you found in Activity 1:

- Is it light, shady or dark?
- Is it wet, damp or dry?
- Is it hot, warm or cold?

What other words can you think of to describe the habitats? Add them to your table.

What temperature did you record in each habitat?

	Where is the habitat?	**Words to describe what the habitat is like**	**Temperature (°C)**
Habitat 1			
Habitat 2			

Compare your table with that of your partner. Add any words that you did not have to your table.

3 Collecting minibeasts

Use the pooter as your teacher showed you. Look under leaves and stones or under fallen leaves on the ground.

How many minibeasts did you catch with the pooter? ___________

Draw one of the minibeasts you found with a pooter.

Describe how you made a pitfall trap. Use words from the box.

fell	hole	time
jar	magnifying glass	

We dug a ___________ in the ground. Then we put a ___________ in the hole. We left the trap for some ___________. We used a ______________________ to look at the minibeasts that ___________ into the jar.

How many minibeasts did you find with your pitfall trap?

____

____

Draw one of the minibeasts you found in your pitfall trap.

Extension

Where do the most minibeasts live?

Draw a bar chart like the one in the Student Book on the grid below. Show how many minibeasts you found in each habitat.

4 **Pond dipping**

You are going to look for some minibeasts in a pond.

Put some water in a plastic tray or box.

Carefully place any minibeasts you collect from the pond into the water in the tray.

Did you find different types of minibeasts in the pond than in the other habitats? Circle your answer.

Yes **No**

Are the conditions in the pond the same or different compared to the other habitats? Circle your answer.

Same **Different**

Draw some of the new minibeasts you found. Write their names if you can.

5 **Matching minibeasts, habitats and conditions**

Think about all the minibeasts you looked at. Choose any two. They need to live in different habitats.

What conditions do they need to live? Write and draw your answers in the table below.

Habitat	Minibeast (write or draw)	What conditions does the minibeast need?

Extension

Why do so many things live on coral reefs?

____

____

____

____

Checklist

Read each sentence and circle a face for it. Like this:

- I understand.
- I understand a bit.
- I need more help to understand this.

- I can name three or more different habitats.
- I can describe conditions in different habitats.
- I can say why different animals live in different habitats.
- I know of different ways to catch minibeasts.

6.2 Caring for the environment

Practising my science language

1 **What do you think?**

Discuss the plans for a new school building in your group.

The questions below will help your ideas.

What would you like a new school to have? A large play area? A good car park? Outdoor football pitches?

What habitats might be damaged or lost?

How can you have a great new school **and** protect the habitats for living things?

Now draw a poster to show what you think the new school should look like.

Show your poster and present your ideas to the rest of the class.

2 **Litter collection**

Complete the sentences.

We found ________ pieces of litter. The whole class found ________ pieces of litter.

We found most litter ____.

What can we do so that there will be less litter?

We can make sure there is less litter by ______________________________

____

____.

Extension

Find out more about organic farming.

Tick the sentences that are true. One has been done for you.

- Organic farming uses chemicals to kill insects. ☐
- Organic farming is good for wildlife. ☑
- Birds can find lots of insects to eat on organic farms. ☐
- Organic farming does not protect the environment. ☐
- Organic farming does not use chemicals to kill weeds. ☐
- Organic farming uses compost. ☐

Look in a shop or a market. What fruit or vegetables come from organic farms?

Draw a picture of one organic fruit or vegetable.

Checklist

Read each sentence and circle a face for it. Like this:

- I understand.
- I understand a bit.
- I need more help to understand this.

- I can describe how humans can damage the environment.
- I can describe how humans can help to protect the environment.

6.3 Weather

Practising my science language

1 Weather words

Here are some weather words.

hot	warm	cold	frosty
snowy	windy	cloudy	icy

Choose two words to describe the weather on a certain day. Write the words on the answer lines.

For example: Cold and windy

__________ and __________

Draw a picture to show what this weather looks like.

2 What is the weather like today?

What is the weather like in the morning? ______________________

____

What is the weather like in the afternoon?______________________

____

Did the weather change during the day? **Yes** **No**

What do you think the weather might be like tomorrow? __________

____

Write two sentences about today's weather here.

____

____

____

3 Making your own weather symbols

Look at your class display of weather symbols.

In the table below, draw the clearest symbol for each type of weather.

Sunny	Windy	Light clouds	Big, heavy clouds
Rainy	**Thunderstorm**	**Mixture of sunny and cloudy**	**Snowy**

4 **My weather record**

Look at the weather record in the Student Book on page 88. Make your own record in the chart below.

Day	Week 1	Week 2
Monday		
Tuesday		
Wednesday		
Thursday		
Friday		
Saturday		
Sunday		

Extension

Record the rainfall measurements below when you record the weather in Activity 4.

Day	Week 1	Week 2
Monday		
Tuesday		
Wednesday		
Thursday		
Friday		
Saturday		
Sunday		

5 Weather patterns

Use your weather record from Activity 4 to draw a bar chart.

You can look at the example on page 89 of your Student Book.

If you found the same type of weather every day, you will need a column 14 spaces high.

Checklist

Read each sentence and circle a face for it. Like this:

I understand.

I understand a bit.

I need more help to understand this.

- I can describe different types of weather.
- I can use symbols and charts to record the weather.

Glossary

In your own language, write down what these words mean:

animal

____

____

cloudy

____

____

cold

____

____

compost

____

____

condition

____

____

environment

____

____

frosty

____

____

habitat

____

____

hot

____

____

icy

____

____

litter

____

____

minibeast

____

____

organic

____

____

plant

____

____

rainy

____

____

snowy

____

____

Glossary

storm

sunny

temperature

thermometer

warm

weather

wet

wildlife

windy